INSIDE MLB

KANSAS CITY ROYALS

Sam Rhodes

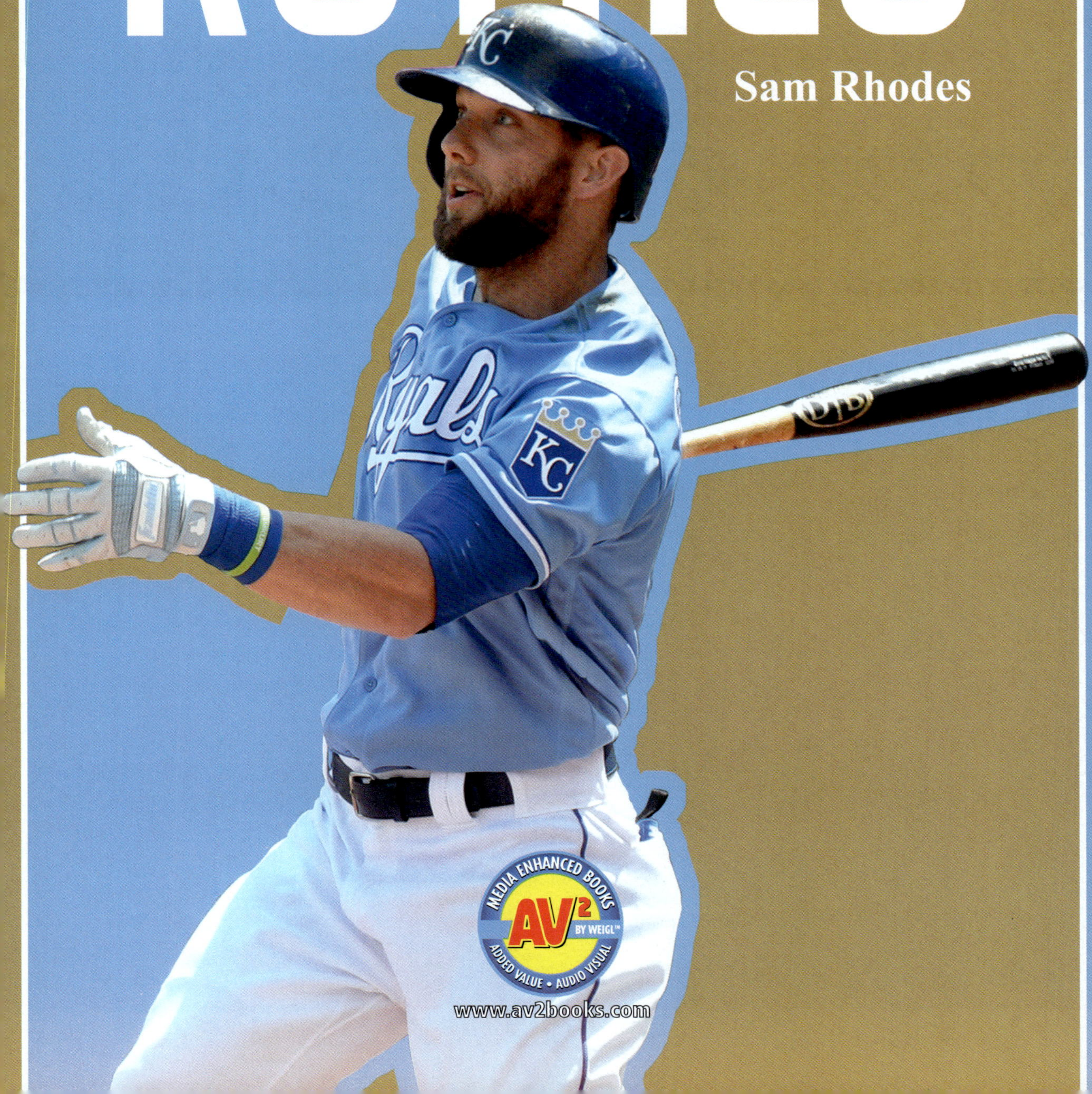

Published by AV² by Weigl
350 5th Avenue, 59th Floor
New York, NY 10118
Website: www.av2books.com

Library of Congress Control Number: 2017963686

ISBN 978-1-4896-7971-0 (hardcover)
ISBN 978-1-4896-7972-7 (softcover)
ISBN 978-1-4896-7973-4 (multi-user eBook)

Printed in the United States of America in Brainerd, Minnesota
1 2 3 4 5 6 7 8 9 0 22 21 20 19 18

012018
120817

Project Coordinator: John Willis Designer: Nick Newton

Every reasonable effort has been made to trace ownership and to obtain permission to reprint copyright material. The publishers would be pleased to have any errors or omissions brought to their attention so that they may be corrected in subsequent printings.

The publisher acknowledges Getty Images, Alamy, and iStock as its primary image suppliers for this title.

INSIDE MLB

Contents

Pitcher Scott Alexander was drafted to the major leagues after high school, but chose not to sign and attended college instead. He was drafted again in 2010, and this time joined the Kansas City Royals.

GO, ROYALS!

Kansas City, Missouri, is proud of its baseball team. Through good seasons and bad, the fans remain fiercely loyal to their team, the Kansas City Royals. The **franchise** is one of the 10 newest baseball clubs, but it has already had many remarkable moments. With notable talent at bat, on the field, and on the mound, the Royals have quickly become an impressive team.

Kansas City, Missouri, neighbors **Kansas City, Kansas**. The two cities are separated by a **state border**.

The Kansas City Royals finished the 2017 season third in their division. They scored more than 700 runs.

Who Are the Royals?

Major League Baseball (MLB) is made up of two leagues: American and National. Each league has East, Central, and West **divisions**. The Kansas City Royals play in the American League (AL) Central Division. After the regular season, the best teams in each division go to the playoffs, or postseason. The Royals have made the playoffs nine times. They have won the **World Series** twice.

Before the **Royals**, Kansas City had another MLB team. The **Kansas City Athletics** played from **1955 to 1967** before moving to Oakland.

Outfielder Bo Jackson played with the Royals from 1986 to 1990. During that time, he also played professional football with the Los Angeles Raiders.

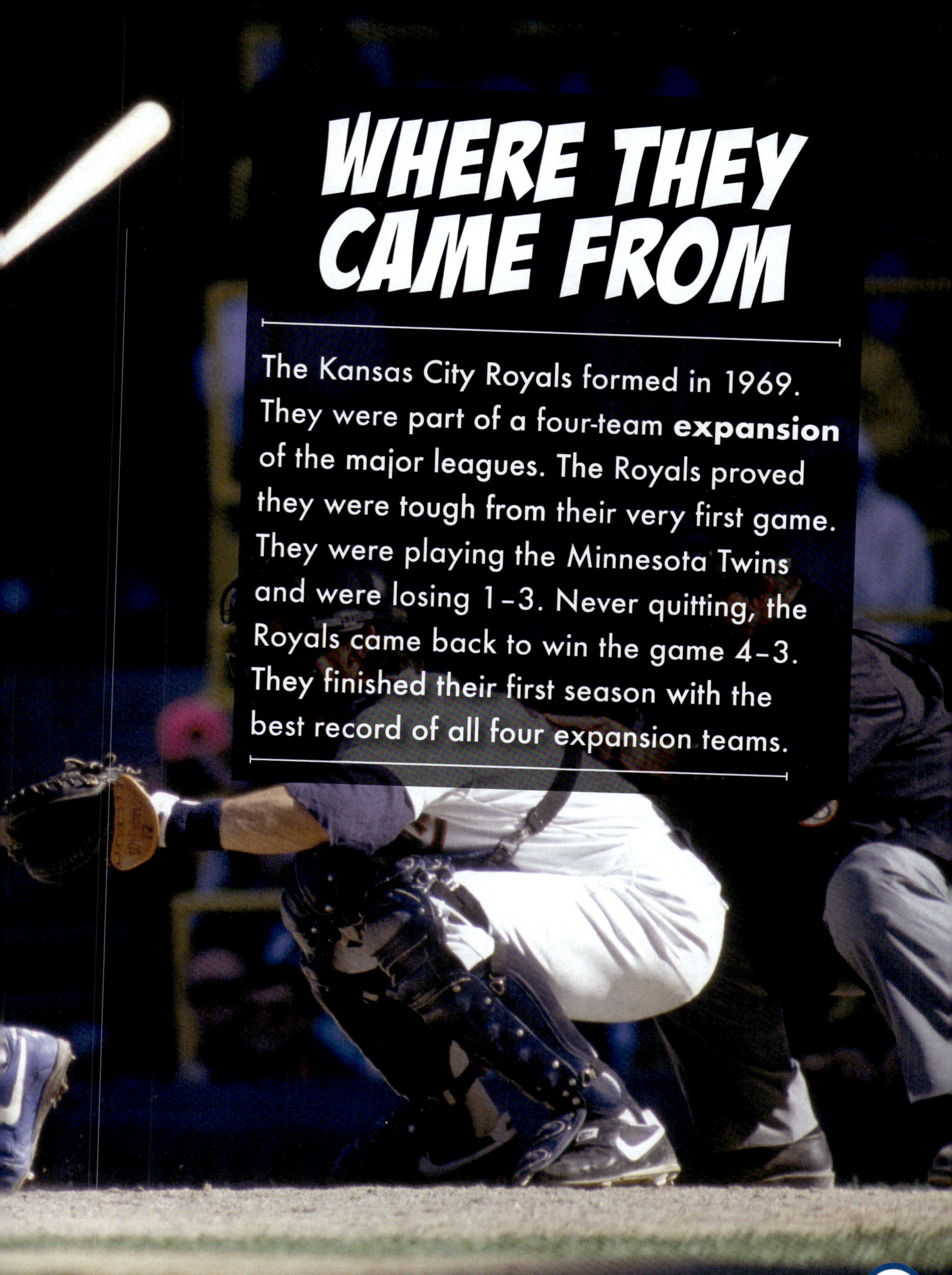

WHERE THEY CAME FROM

The Kansas City Royals formed in 1969. They were part of a four-team **expansion** of the major leagues. The Royals proved they were tough from their very first game. They were playing the Minnesota Twins and were losing 1–3. Never quitting, the Royals came back to win the game 4–3. They finished their first season with the best record of all four expansion teams.

Despite many great plays by Royals players, including second baseman Whit Merrifield, the team lost all four 2017 matchups against their rivals, the Cardinals.

Who They Play

The Kansas City Royals play 162 games in the regular season. They play 76 of those games against other teams in the AL Central Division. Those teams are the Detroit Tigers, the Cleveland Indians, the Minnesota Twins, and the Chicago White Sox. The Royals' biggest **rivals** are the St. Louis Cardinals. Being in different divisions, they do not play each other often. But when they do, sparks fly!

The **Royals** were in the **AL West Division** until **1994**, when they moved to the newly created **AL Central Division**.

Where They Play

Kauffman Stadium is home to the Kansas City Royals. It opened in April 1973 as Royal Stadium. In 1993, it was renamed Kauffman Stadium in honor of Ewing Kauffman, the first owner of the team. The ballpark was renovated in 2009. New additions included solar panels that provide electricity for the stadium year-round. The park seats 37,903 fans.

Since opening in **1973**, **Kauffman Stadium** has hosted close to **80 million** spectators.

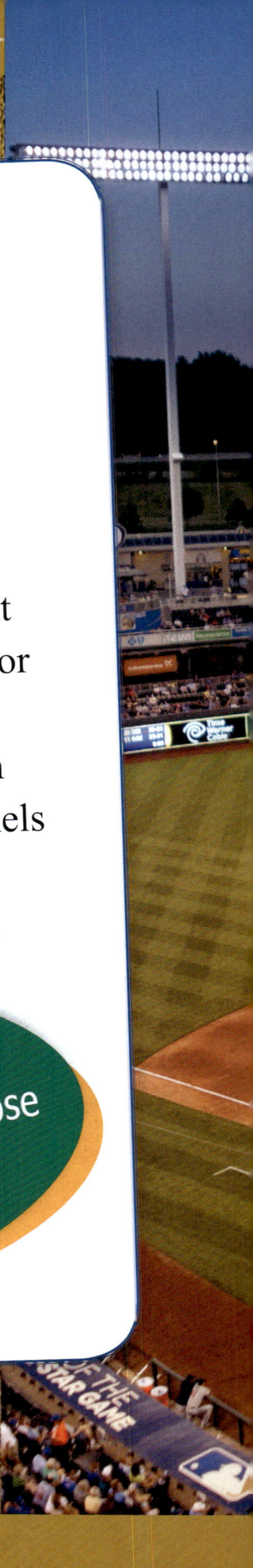

At home games, the Royals have a tradition of playing the song "Friends in Low Places" by Garth Brooks.

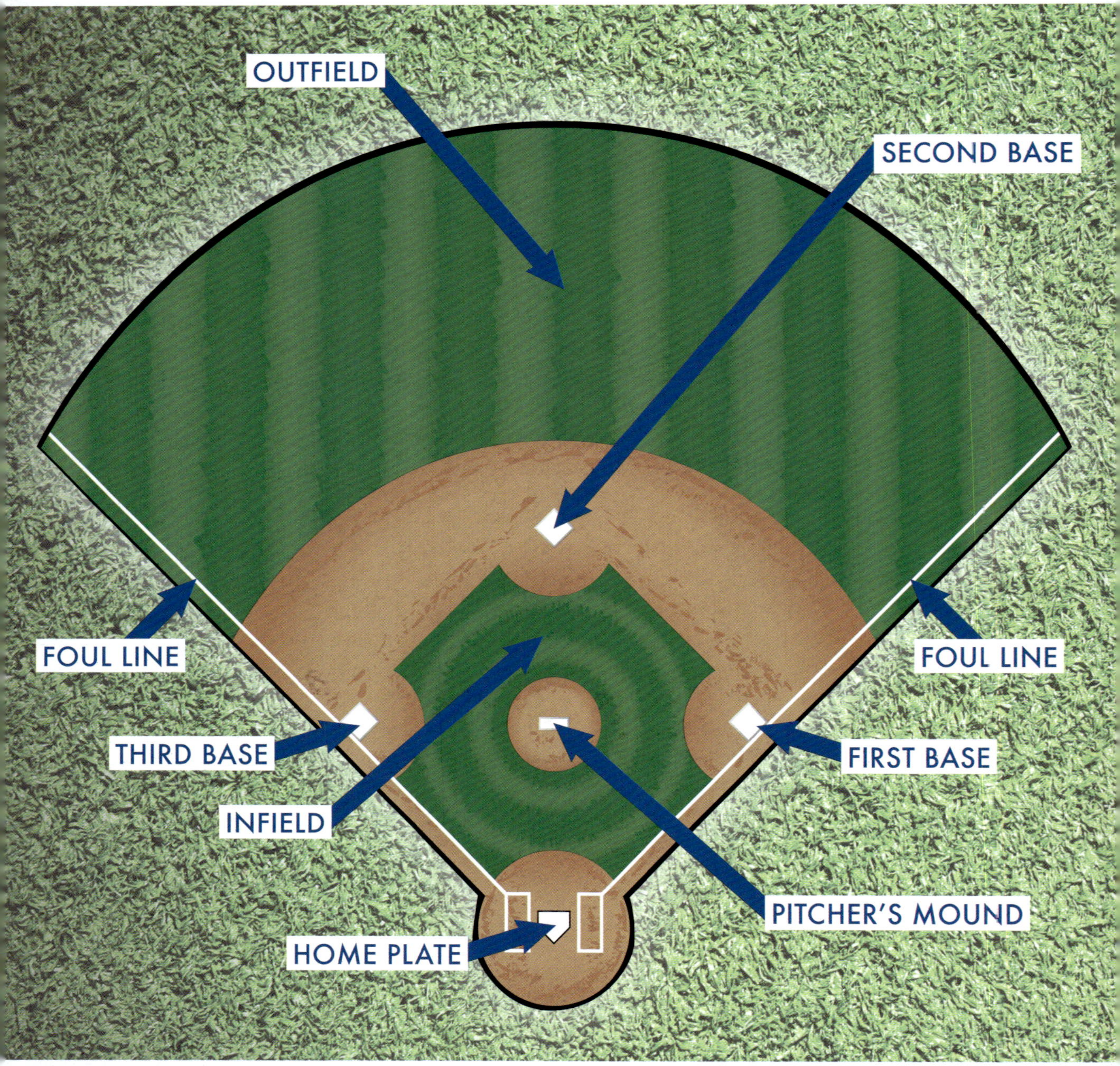
OUTFIELD
SECOND BASE
FOUL LINE
FOUL LINE
THIRD BASE
FIRST BASE
INFIELD
PITCHER'S MOUND
HOME PLATE

THE BASEBALL DIAMOND

Baseball games are played on a field called a diamond. Four bases form this diamond shape. The bases are 90 feet (27 meters) apart. The area around and between the bases is called the infield. At the center of the infield is the pitcher's mound. The grass area beyond the bases is called the outfield. White lines start at **home plate** and go toward the outfield. These are the foul lines. Baseballs hit outside these lines are out of play unless a fielder catches them. The outfield walls are about 300–450 feet (91–137 m) from home plate.

Big Days

Over the years, the Kansas City Royals have had some incredible wins. Here are some of their finest seasons:

1976: *For Royals fans, the first seven seasons were tough. The team came in fourth or fifth in their division most years. Then, in the 1976 season, Kansas City won 90 games and their first division* ***title****. They lost in the playoffs, but this was a big step for the young team.*

1985: *The Royals made it to the World Series in 1985. They faced the St. Louis Cardinals. After four games, the Royals were down three games to one. They came back, winning three games straight and taking their first World Series* ***championship****.*

2015: *In 2014, the Royals lost the World Series by one game. The 2015 season opened with high hopes. They won their division, cruised through the playoffs, then beat the New York Mets, winning their first World Series in 30 years.*

Many of the 2015 Royals players have nicknames. First baseman Eric Hosmer is known as "Papo." Third baseman Mike Moustakas is nicknamed "Moose."

Right fielder Norichika Aoki grounded out against the Texas Rangers during an August 2014 away game. The Royals lost 1–3.

Tough Days

The Royals have also had their share of heartbreak as a baseball club. These are some of their most difficult seasons:

1978: *After struggling as a new team, the Royals were hungry for victory. In 1978, they finally made the playoffs. The only thing in the way of their first World Series was the New York Yankees. The Royals fought hard, but they lost the American League Championship Series to the Yankees, three games to one.*

2001: *The Royals finished in last place in their division, with 65 wins and 97 losses. It was the seventh season in a row they lost more than half of their games. At this point, they had not made the playoffs in 15 years.*

2014: *With no postseason appearances, the Royals finally made it to the playoffs. The Royals swept the Los Angeles Angels three games to zero, then the Baltimore Orioles four games to zero. Despite their momentum, they lost the World Series to the San Francisco Giants.*

Royals mascot Sluggerrr's favorite songs are "Welcome to the Jungle" and "The Lion Sleeps Tonight."

MEET THE FANS

Fans of the Kansas City Royals are always there for their team. They follow players on **social media** to show support even during the off-season. Visiting Kauffman Stadium is the best way to cheer on the Royals. Fans will find Sluggerrr the lion at every home game. Sluggerrr is the Royals' mascot. He loves dancing on the dugout and hanging out with Royals fans.

During his nine seasons with the Royals, Freddie Patek earned 182 doubles, 41 triples, and 28 home runs.

Bret Saberhagen, Pitcher

Heroes Then...

Many exceptional players have worn the Royals jersey. Shortstop Freddie Patek moved to Kansas City in 1971. An all-around great player, he led the league in triples and double plays that year. Amos Otis was one of the best center fielders in baseball. In 1971, he stole five bases in one game. He was the first player to do that since 1927. Pitcher Charlie Leibrandt helped the 1985 Royals win the World Series. Bret Saberhagen was named the World Series **Most Valuable Player (MVP)** in 1985. He pitched a **shutout** game against the Cardinals. George Brett was selected for the **All-Star Game** team every year from 1976 to 1988. In 1976, he ranked first in singles, second in doubles, first in triples, and first in batting average in the American League. Frank White was an outstanding second baseman who won the **Gold Glove Award** eight times between 1977 and 1987.

Heroes Now...

Today, the Kansas City Royals team is loaded with talent. Center fielder Lorenzo Cain made the All-Star team in 2015. He helped the Royals win the World Series that same year. Eric Hosmer won the Gold Glove Award as a first baseman every year from 2013 to 2015. Danny Duffy pitches for the Royals. In one game in August 2016, he struck out 16 batters, setting a new franchise record. Second baseman Whit Merrifield led the American League in stolen bases in 2017. Mike Moustakas, the Royals' third baseman, cranked out 38 home runs in the regular season. That was the fifth highest in the American League in 2017. Royals catcher Salvador Pérez ranked first in assists as catcher in 2013, 2015, and 2016. He was also chosen as the World Series MVP in 2015.

The present-day Royals are loaded with star players.

Lorenzo Cain, Outfielder

Eric Hosmer, First Baseman

Danny Duffy, Pitcher

GEARING UP

Baseball players all wear a team jersey and pants. They have to wear a team hat in the field and a helmet when batting. Take a look at Salvador Pérez and Eric Hosmer to see some other parts of a baseball player's uniform.

Salvador Pérez, Catcher

BATTING HELMET
TEAM JERSEY
BATTING GLOVES
BAT
TEAM PANTS
BASEBALL CLEATS
Eric Hosmer,
First Baseman

SPORTS STATS

Here are some all-time career records for the Kansas City Royals. All of the stats are through the 2017 season.

A Major League baseball weighs about **5 ounces** (142 grams). It is **9 inches** (23 centimeters) around. A leather cover surrounds **hundreds** of feet of string. That string is wound around a small center of **rubber** and **cork**.

Home Runs

George Brett, **317**

Mike Sweeney, **197**

Runs Batted In

George Brett, **1,596**

Hal McRae, **1,012**

Batting Average

Jose Offerman, **.306**

George Brett, **.305**

Stolen Bases

Willie Wilson, **612**

Amos Otis, **340**

Wins by a Pitcher

Paul Splittorff, **166**

Dennis Leonard, **144**

Wins by a Manager

Ned Yost, **629**

Whitey Herzog, **410**

Earned Run Average

Dan Quisenberry, **2.55**

Steve Farr, **3.05**

Quiz

1 How many times have the Royals made the playoffs?

2 When were the Royals formed?

3 Who are the Royals' biggest rivals?

4 How far apart are the bases on the baseball diamond?

5 In what year did the Royals win their first World Series in 30 years?

6 Who pitched a shutout game against the Cardinals in 1985?

7 When do players have to wear a helmet?

8 Which Royals manager has the most wins?

Answers

1. Nine
2. 1969
3. The St. Louis Cardinals
4. 90 feet (27 m)
5. 2015
6. Bret Saberhagen
7. When batting
8. Ned Yost

Key Words

All-Star Game: an annual midseason game in which the best players from the AL and NL play against each other

championship: one or more games that decide which team is the best

divisions: groups of teams that form one part of a professional sports league

expansion: in baseball, the addition of new teams

franchise: a team that belongs to a professional sports league

Gold Glove Award: an annual award given to a player from each defensive position in each league

home plate: the base where a batter stands and where a runner must touch to score a run

Most Valuable Player (MVP): an annual award given to one player from each league

rivals: teams that have a strong sense of competition with each other

shutout: a game in which one team is kept from scoring

social media: websites that people use to share messages, information, and ideas with each other

title: a championship

World Series: an annual series played between the champions of each league

Index

Log on to www.av2books.com

AV² by Weigl brings you media enhanced books that support active learning. Go to www.av2books.com, and enter the special code found on page 2 of this book. You will gain access to enriched and enhanced content that supplements and complements this book. Content includes video, audio, weblinks, quizzes, a slide show, and activities.

AV² Online Navigation

Audio
Listen to sections of the book read aloud.

Book Pages
AV² pages directly correspond to pages in the book.

Video
Watch informative video clips.

Embedded Weblinks
Gain additional information for research.

Key Words
Study vocabulary, and complete a matching word activity.

Try This!
Complete activities and hands-on experiments.

Quizzes
Test your knowledge.

Slide Show
View images and captions, and prepare a presentation.

AV² was built to bridge the gap between print and digital. We encourage you to tell us what you like and what you want to see in the future.

Sign up to be an AV² Ambassador at www.av2books.com/ambassador.

Due to the dynamic nature of the Internet, some of the URLs and activities provided as part of AV² by Weigl may have changed or ceased to exist. AV² by Weigl accepts no responsibility for any such changes. All media enhanced books are regularly monitored to update addresses and sites in a timely manner. Contact AV² by Weigl at 1-866-649-3445 or av2books@weigl.com with any questions, comments, or feedback.